RECIPES
from Dobromyl

RECIPES
from Dobromyl

Friends
The Summer English Camp

AN ARTHUR KURZWEIL BOOK
New York/Jerusalem

Copyright © 2019 by Arthur Kurzweil

All rights reserved

AN ARTHUR KURZWEIL BOOK
New York/Jerusalem

arthurkurzweilbooks.com

First edition

ISBN: 978-1-7321749-1-7

To the children of Dobromyl:
May you
grow up
strong and righteous.

Contents

Foreword by Arthur Kurzweil ... 1

My Native Town by Olexandra Mrachynska ... 3

Soups ... 5
    Sorrel Soup ... 7
    Borscht (*Borshch*) ... 8
    Green Borscht (*Borshch*) with Sorrel ... 10
    Soup with Sauerkraut Brine (*Kvasivka*) ... 11

Salads ... 13
    Beet Root Salad with Horseradish ... 15
    Vegetable Salad ... 16
    Dniester Salad ... 17
    Vinaigrette Salad ... 18

Breads ... 19
    Garlic Rolls (*Pampushky*) ... 21
    Easter Bread ... 22

Pierogi (*Varenyky*) ... 25
    Pierogi Recipe #1 ... 27
    Pierogi Recipe #2 ... 28
    Pierogi with Sour Cabbage ... 30

Traditional Ukrainian Vegetarian Dishes ... 33
    Potato Pancake (*Deruny*) ... 35

Cabbage Rolls (*Holubtsi*)	*36*
Sauteed Cabbage with Peas	37
Cornmeal with Sour Cream (*Hutsul Banush*)	38
Mushrooms with Sauce	39
Omelet	40
Traditional Ukrainian Meat Dishes	**41**
Rice Pilaf (*Plov*)	43
Fried Chicken	44
Chicken Kiev	45
Marinated Baked Ham	46
Pork Rolls Filled with Mushrooms	47
Traditional Ukrainian Fish Dishes	**49**
Dressed Herring	51
Herring	52
Pizza	**53**
Pizza Recipe #1	55
Pizza Recipe #2	56
Pizza Recipe #3	57
Donuts	**59**
Donut Recipe #1	61
Donut Recipe #2	62
Donut Recipe #3	64
Desserts	**65**
Cottage Cheese Pancakes (*Symyky*)	67
Charlotke	68
Pumpkin Dough	69
Fruit Ice Cream	70
Ice Cream	71

Holiday Recipes	73
Traditional Beverage (*Uzvar*)	75
Cereal Dish #1 (*Kutya*)	76
Cereal Dish #2 (*Kutya*)	77
Cereal Dish #3 (*Kutya*)	78
Mushroom and Onion Dumplings (*Vushka*)	79
Sugar Cookies	80

Foreword

Улітку 2018 року я брав участь у напруженому, але водночас захопливому тижні з Олександрою Мрачинською, вчителькою англійської мови з Добромиля, яка цілковито віддана своїй справі, та вісімнадцятьма її учнями.

Для мене немає нічого прекраснішого, ніж обличчя молодих людей, очі яких випромінюють жагу до знань. Упродовж тижня учні завзято працювали над удосконаленням своїх навичок володіння англійською мовою.

Одним із наших проектів стало створення української кулінарної книги англійською мовою. Кожен учень відправився додому, а наступного дня повернувся до нашого "англійського табору" із одним або кількома традиційними українськими рецептами.

Кожен рецепт мав свій унікальний стиль; їх залишено без редагування та перевірки.

Смачного!

Окрему подяку хочу висловити Юрію Петрику, Галині Луцишин, Катажині Сосновській, Олександрі Мрачинській, Венді Бернштайн та Джудіт Таллі.

— Артур Керзвайл

In the summer of 2018, I participated in an intensive yet enjoyable week with Olexandra Mrachynska, a dedicated English teacher in Dobromyl, and 18 of her students.

For me, there is nothing more beautiful than the faces of young people who are eager to learn. In this case, the enthusiastic students were improving their English language skills.

As one of the projects during our week together, we decided to create a Ukrainian cookbook — in English. Each student went home and came back to "English camp" the next day with one or more Ukrainian recipes.

All of the recipes are untested. Each is written in its own unedited style.

Enjoy!

Special thanks go to Petryk Yurij, Halia Lutsyshyn, Katarzyna Sosnowska, Olexandra Mrachynska, Wendy Bernstein, and Judith Tulli.

— Arthur Kurzweil
February 2019

My Native Town

*There are a lot of cities,
Beautiful and fine.
But the town I like best
Is no doubt mine.*

It is said that every town, like every person, has its own character, soul, and destiny. Wherever you live, you'll remember your Motherland. It may be a town, a city, or a small village. Wherever you live, work, or travel, you'll always try to return to the place where you spent your childhood. Your native place seems to be the dearest and the best place in the whole world.

So, I'd like to tell you about one of them. It is Dobromyl, my native town. It stands on the green hills above the river of Vyrva. You see, our town is one of the oldest in Western Ukraine. It was founded in 1374. Dobromyl was granted the Magdeburg right many years ago.

There are some places of interest near my town. I can suggest that you visit a castle of the old Herburt dynasty and the Monastery. But, unfortunately, the castle was ruined by wars and people; only walls are left. The place where the Monastery is situated is simply marvelous. It was built in 1705.

Dobromyl is a center of three cultures: Ukrainian, Polish, and Jewish. The statue of the great Polish poet Adam Mitskevich and the Jewish cemetery should also be mentioned.

My town is a cultural center because you can see a modern school, a liceum (high school), the House of Prosvita, a musical school, a kindergarten, and libraries for children and adults.

The center of Dobromyl is famous for its Rynok Square. One can see an ancient municipal building called Ratusha, with a clock tower on the top. The Town Council is in the building now.

To my mind a modern playground is the most attractive place where children and their parents can spend free time. This place is a gift for the children from the Kurzweil family.

Frankly speaking, many hard-working and talented people live in my town. I should say that I like my native town greatly and will always be proud of it. In Dobromyl I spent my childhood, went to school, hoped, and dreamed. That's why I have chosen this place for living and working.

— *Olexandra Mrachynska*
September 2018

Soups

Sorrel Soup

Submitted by Olexandra Mrachynska

This soup is made in the Spring. Sometimes people call sorrel soup green borscht.

Ingredients

- 6 medium potatoes
- 1 carrot
- 4 eggs
- 1 medium onion
- 4 cups fresh chopped sorrel
- 2 tbsp fresh chopped dill
- 2 bay leaves
- 2 liters water
- parsley to taste
- salt to taste
- pepper to taste
- 2 tbsp oil
- Fennel to taste
- Sour cream

Stages of Cooking

1. Fill a large pot with 2 liters of water.
2. Add diced potatoes, 2 bay leaves, and lightly boil for 15 minutes.
3. While potatoes are cooking, sauté chopped onion in oil over medium heat until golden brown. Add to the pot. Boil eggs and dice them. Add to the pot.
4. When potatoes are cooked through, stir in sorrel and dill. Bring pot to a boil and simmer an additional 3 to 5 minutes, or until sorrel is soft.
5. Serve hot with sour cream.

Borscht (*Borshch*)

Submitted by Oleh Manko

This recipe was given by my grandmother, Mariya Manko. I like cooking with my grandmother very much. My favorite dish is borscht. It consists of the following ingredients:

Ingredients

- 2-3 potatoes
- Beet roots
- Cabbage
- Carrots
- 1 onion
- 2-3 cloves garlic
- 1 bay leaf
- 1 pepper
- Tomatoes to taste
- 1 tablespoon cream
- 1 teaspoon vinegar
- Salt to taste
- Dill to taste
- Parsley to taste

Stages of Cooking

1. Cut the cabbage, potatoes, and carrots and put them in a saucepan.
2. Boil for 10 minutes.
3. Then chop the beet roots and add them to the vegetables.
4. Continue boiling.
5. Warm up some butter in a frying pan.
6. Chop the onion and fry it until it becomes yellow.
7. Add some cream and mashed tomatoes.

8. Pour everything into the pot.
9. Add some vinegar and salt.
10. Cut some parsley and dill and put them on a plate before serving.

Green Borscht (*Borshch*) with Sorrel

Submitted by Anastasia Pynylo

This is my Grandmother Luba's recipe. Bon Appetit!

Ingredients

- 2 liters (2 qts) water
- 300 gms (10.5 oz) potatoes
- 300 gms (10.5 oz) chicken
- 150 gms (5 oz) sorrel
- 1 onion
- 1 carrot
- 2 eggs
- Salt and black pepper to taste
- Sour cream to taste

Stages of Cooking

1. Wash and cut sorrel.
2. Cut the carrots into straw-size pieces.
3. Cut the onion in half.
4. Cut the potatoes into cubes.
5. Cook the eggs and cut them into cubes.
6. Rinse the chicken, fill a pot with water, and boil the chicken.
7. Put in the potatoes and cook until half-ready.
8. Bake onion and carrot on low heat.
9. Add the vegetables to the broth and cook until the potatoes are ready.
10. Add the sorrel and warm up for 1 minute.
11. Add eggs, salt, and black pepper.
12. When serving, add sour cream.

Soup with Sauerkraut Brine (*Kvasivka*)

Submitted by Ada Bilousova

This is my grandmother's recipe.

Ingredients

- 500 gms (1 lb) sauerkraut
- 2 to 3 tablespoons sour cream
- 2 to 3 tablespoons flour
- 1 onion
- 5 to 10 tablespoons oil
- Salt to taste
- Pepper to taste

Stages of Cooking

1. Boil the sauerkraut.
2. Sprinkle the salt.
3. Sprinkle sour cream with flour.
4. Stir mixture of sour cream and flour.
5. Pour it into boiling juice of sauerkraut.
6. Fry onion with oil
7. Add salt and pepper.
8. Stir.

Salads

Beet Root Salad with Horseradish

Submitted by Olexandra Mrachynska

Ingredients

- 950 gms (2 lbs) beet root
- 150 gms (5.3 oz) horseradish root
- 50 gms (2 oz) vinegar
- 50 gms (2 oz) sugar
- Salt and ground black pepper to taste

Stages of Cooking

1. Cook the beet root until tender; allow to cool.
2. Peel the beet root and grate coarsely.
3. Peel and finely grate the horseradish.
4. Combine all ingredients, season with salt and pepper to taste. Stir well.

Vegetable Salad

Submitted by Olexandra Mrachynska

This light vegetable salad will compliment any meat dish.

Ingredients

- 200 gms (7 oz) *fresh cucumber*
- 200 gms (7 oz) *sweet pepper*
- 200 gms (7 oz) *tomatoes*
- 30 gms (1 oz) *spring onions*
- 30 gms (1 oz) *any green vegetable*
- 2 tsp *oil*
- Salt and ground black pepper to taste

Stages of Cooking

1. Cut the cucumbers and tomatoes into large pieces.
2. Shred the sweet pepper.
3. Chop the spring onions and herbs.
4. Combine all vegetables, season with salt and pepper.
5. Add the oil; mix well.

Dniester Salad

Submitted by Olexandra Mrachynska

Ingredients

- 400 gms (14 oz) cabbage
- Salt
- 300 gms (10.5 oz) smoked sausage
- 1 can green peas, drained
- 200 gms (7 oz) mayonnaise

Stages of Cooking

1. Finely chop the cabbage.
2. Lightly salt the cabbage, then squeeze to release some liquid.
3. Shred the sausage.
4. Combine all the ingredients and dress the salad with mayonnaise.

Vinaigrette Salad

Submitted by Erast Koliasa

All of our family loves to gather together in the evenings at the kitchen table to drink tea or coffee and to taste Mother's dishes. I like Mother's Vinaigrette Salad. My mother is Natalia Koliasa.

Ingredients

- 3 potatoes
- 3 carrots
- 2-3 beet roots
- 3 pickled cucumbers
- 150 gms (5 oz) canned green peas
- Salt to taste
- Pepper to taste
- 2 tablespoons oil

Stages of Cooking

1. Wash the potatoes, carrots, and beet roots and put them in a saucepan; add water and put the pan on the stove.
2. Bring to a boil and cook until ready.
3. Cool the vegetables completely.
4. Peel the vegetables.
5. Drain off the water from the can of green peas.
6. Cut potatoes, carrots, cucumbers, and beet root into square pieces.
7. Put everything in a salad bowl and add green peas.
8. Salt to your taste and add some oil.
9. Mix everything carefully.
10. Tasty Vinaigrette Salad is ready.

Breads

Garlic Rolls (*Pampushky*)

Submitted by Solomia Hyz

Pampushky are served with borscht.

Ingredients

- 12 gms yeast
- 12 gms sugar
- 8 gms salt
- 225 ml warm water
- 400 gms flour, divided
- 1 egg
- 30 gms (1 oz) garlic
- 50 gms (1.5 oz) oil
- 1 bunch parsley

Stages of Cooking

1. Combine the yeast, sugar, salt, 100 gms of flour, and warm water. Knead the dough and put it aside to ferment.
2. Add the remaining flour and knead the dough well. Set aside to ferment again.
3. Cut the dough into small equal pieces. Powder them with flour and shape into balls.
4. Put the balls on a greased baking tray and let them rest for 20 minutes. Preheat oven to 200c degrees.
5. Brush the dough balls with beaten egg and bake for 20-25 minutes.
6. While the donuts are baking, combine the garlic with the oil and parsley.
7. Brush the finished donuts with garlic sauce.

Easter Bread

Submitted by Ruslan Danko

This recipe was given to me by my granny, Olha Danko.

Ingredients

- 500-600 gms (17.5-21 oz) flour
- 200 gms (7 oz) milk
- 150-200 gms (5-7 oz) butter, melted
- 200 gms (7 oz) sugar, divided
- 4 eggs
- Zest of 1 lemon
- 40-60 gms (1.5-2 oz) pressed yeast
- 150 gms (5 oz) raisins, optional
- 50 gms (1.5 oz) dry almonds, optional
- 20 gms (3/4 oz) vanilla sugar
- Pinch of salt

Stages of Cooking

1. Dissolve yeast in milk.
2. Add a tablespoon of sugar, gradually add in 150-200 gms (5-7 oz) of sifted flour.
3. Beat well until smooth.
4. Cover and let the batter rise in a warm place for an hour.
5. When the batter is ready, add the beaten eggs, remaining sugar, melted butter, lemon zest, and pinch of salt. Mix thoroughly.
6. Add the remaining flour and mix until the dough is neither too soft nor too stiff.
7. If using raisins and almonds, add them in now.
8. Knead until the dough no longer sticks to the hand (at least 10 minutes by hand).
9. Place the dough in a greased bowl, cover the bowl with a tea towel, and put it in a warm place for 1-1.5 hours.

10. Generously grease the pans for baking.
11. Divide the dough into as many parts as you have pans to be filled 1/3 full.
12. Preheat the oven to 350 degrees, then lower the temperature to 210-240 degrees and bake 40-50 minutes.
13. To prevent the tops from over-browning, you may put large pieces of aluminum foil over the bread.
14. Remove the Easter Bread from the oven and let cool in pans for 5 minutes. Then gently remove from the pans onto a towel. Dust with vanilla sugar before serving.

Pierogi

Pierogi Recipe #1 (*Varenyky*)

Submitted by Olexandra Mrachynska

Varenyky is a popular national Ukrainian dish, not a festive dish.

Ingredients

Dough
- 320-350 gms flour
- 2 eggs
- Salt to taste
- 250 ml water or milk

Filling
- 10-14 potatoes
- 2 or 3 fried onions
- Salt to taste
- Pepper to taste
- 2 tablespoons vegetable oil

Stages of Cooking

1. Add eggs to the flour.
2. Pour in the water or milk and knead until it becomes smooth.
3. Add salt and knead.
4. Form a ball.
5. Using a rolling pin, roll out the dough to a very thin sheet.
6. Take a glass and cut out circles in the prepared dough.
7. For the potato filling, prepare the potato puree and mix it with chopped and fried onion.
8. Add salt and pepper to taste.

Pierogi Recipe #2 (*Varenyky*)

Submitted by Iryna Denys

This recipe was given to me by my mother, Natalia Denys. Pierogis are small pastries made from unleavened dough with a variety of fillings — berries, farmer cheese, cheese, potatoes, and other things. They are boiled and served with sour cream, sugar, and butter.

Ingredients

Filling

- 500 gms (1 lb) *tvorog* (farmer cheese)
- 2 eggs
- 50 gms (1.5 oz) sugar
- Salt to taste

Dough

- 300 gms (10.5 oz) flour
- 1 egg
- 150 gms (5 oz) water

- Sour cream and sugar, for serving

Stages of Cooking

1. Filling:
    a. Combine the farmer cheese, eggs, sugar, and salt.
    b. Run through a sieve.
2. Dough:
    a. Combine water, egg, and flour. Knead, adding more flour if needed, and roll out finely.
    b. Make round cutout from a glass or cup.
    c. Put the filling in the center of every round.

    d.   Pinch the edges to close.
3. Cook in lightly boiling salted water until pierogis are on the surface.
4. Serve with sugar and sour cream.

Pierogi (*Varenyky*) with Sour Cabbage

Submitted by Mary Sydir

This is my grandmother's family recipe for pierogi. Enjoy your meal!

Ingredients

- 1 egg
- 1 onion
- 2-3 cups wheat flour
- 5 gms (1 teaspoon) salt, plus more to taste
- 4 tbsp sunflower oil, divided
- 150 gms (5 oz) sour cabbage
- Black ground pepper to taste
- Sour cream to taste
- Nutmeg to taste
- 1 cup milk or water

Stages of Cooking

Stuffing
1. Put sour cabbage in a pan, pour in water, and boil until soft.
2. Place the cabbage in a colander and let drain.
3. Cool the cabbage and set aside.
4. Peel the onion, dice it, and sauté in 1 tbsp sunflower oil.
5. Add the cabbage, nutmeg, and salt and black pepper to taste. Stir the ingredients.

Dough
1. Gradually combine flour, salt, warm water, and egg.
2. Thoroughly mix everything.
3. Pour in 3 tbsp of sunflower oil.
4. Knead the dough for one minute.

5. Place the prepared dough in the refrigerator for 30 minutes.
6. Roll out the dough.
7. Take a cup and cut out circles.
8. Put the cabbage stuffing in each circle.
9. Fold the dough over to cover the stuffing and crimp the edges.
10. Repeat the procedure until you use all the dough and the cabbage stuffing.
11. Cover the prepared pierogis with a napkin and leave for a while.
12. Boil pierogis in salted water.
13. Transfer the cooked pierogis to a plate and serve with sour cream.

Traditional Ukrainian Vegeterian Dishes

Potato Pancake (*Deruny*)

Submitted by Olexandra Mrachynska

Ingredients

- 500 gms (1 lb) potatoes
- 100 gms (3.5 oz) sour cream
- ½ tsp ground black pepper
- 1 tsp salt
- 2 eggs
- 3 tbsp flour
- 100 ml (3.5 oz) vegetable oil

Stages of Cooking

1. Peel and wash the potatoes. Grate the potatoes to a medium texture.
2. Combine the grated potatoes with salt, pepper, eggs, and flour. Stir until completely combined.
3. Heat vegetable oil in a frying pan. Add potato mixture in spoonfuls and fry each side until they are golden.
4. Serve the potato pancakes with sour cream.

Cabbage Rolls (*Holubtsi*)

Submitted by Erast Koliasa

I love my grandmother. Her food is tasty but most of all I like Grandma's cabbage rolls. My grandmother is Romania Stepaniak.

Ingredients

- 1 medium cabbage, core removed
- 1 onion, finely grated
- 1 carrot, shredded
- 5 tbsp oil
- 10 medium-sized potatoes, finely grated
- 2 tsp salt

Stages of Cooking

1. Add cabbage to a pot of boiling water, core down, and cook for 10 minutes.
2. Carefully remove 4 or 5 leaves, allowing cabbage to simmer for an additional 5 minutes. Remove another 4 or 5 leaves. Allow cabbage to simmer for an additional 5 minutes after each set of leaves is removed.
3. Finely grate the potatoes, onion, and carrot.
4. Add oil and salt to the onion, carrot, and potatoes and mix.
5. *How to Roll the Smaller Leaves of the Cabbage:* Slice off the bump of the core and place 2-3 heaping tablespoons of the potato mixture into each leaf. Roll carefully, folding in the sides; stack rolls in a pot.
6. *How to Roll the Large Leaves of the Cabbage:* Remove the middle of the stem, cutting leaf into two portions. Place 2 tablespoons of the filling onto the bottom part of the leaf and roll, folding in the sides. Stack in a pot.
7. Pour water evenly over the top, then put the pan on the hob (stove).
8. Bring to a boil and cook until ready (approximately 40 to 60 minutes).

Sauteed Cabbage with Peas

Submitted by Sofia Ledakhivska

Prepared for the Holy Supper, this is the recipe from my grandmother.

Ingredients

- 2 cups peas
- 1 kg (2 lbs) cabbage
- 1 large onion
- Sunflower and linseed oil

Stages of Cooking

1. Boil the peas.
2. Boil the cabbage.
3. In a large bowl, mix the cabbage and peas.
4. Finely cut the onion and fry in sunflower and linseed oil.
5. Add onion to cabbage and peas.
6. Mix everything gently.

Cornmeal with Sour Cream (*Hutsul Banush*)

Submitted by Solomia Hyz

Ingredients

- 300 gms (10.5 oz) mushrooms
- 1 tbsp oil
- 200 gms (7 oz) pork belly (salo)
- 300 gms (10.5 oz) sheep cheese (bryndza)
- 3 cups sour cream
- 1 cup cornmeal grits
- Salt and black pepper to taste

Stages of Cooking

1. Chop the mushrooms and fry in oil until browned. Set aside.
2. Chop or grate the cheese. Set aside.
3. Finely chop the pork and fry over medium heat until crisp, pouring off the fat occasionally. Set aside.
4. Boil the sour cream in a large pot. Slowly add the cornmeal, stirring continuously to avoid lumps.
5. Reduce the heat to low and stir continuously until the cornmeal is very thick.
6. Place the cornmeal in bowls and top with cheese, mushrooms, and pork belly.

Mushrooms with Sauce

Submitted by Ylia Chura

This is my mom's recipe.

Ingredients

- 50-80 gms (1 1/2-3 oz) dried white mushrooms
- 1 onion
- 1 tbsp flour
- 2-3 tbsp sunflower oil
- Salt and black pepper to taste
- 1 cup milk

Stages of Cooking

1. Soak dried mushrooms in water and leave for 3 to 4 hours or overnight.
2. Drain mushrooms in a colander and wash them well.
3. Place mushrooms in 500-600 ml (17-20 oz) water, bring to a boil, cover, and cook on low heat for 1 hour.
4. Peel the onion and cut into small cubes. In a pan of sunflower oil, fry the onion to a clear state, stirring from time to time.
5. Drain mushrooms, reserving the broth. Rinse mushrooms and cut or grind thoroughly. Strain the broth through a sieve or gauze (folded several times).
6. Add mushrooms, onion, and salt; fry on a low fire for 15 minutes, stirring occasionally.
7. In a dry frying pan on a low fire, fry the flour to a barely brown color, stirring the whole time.
8. Gradually add milk to the roasted flour until you get a thick, smooth mass, stirring the entire time so that no lumps form.
9. Add fried flour to mushrooms and mix thoroughly. Boil only 1 minute.

Omelet

Submitted by Katya Voloshyn

My grandmother's name is Dariya. She is very hardworking and cooks well. My favorite dish is her omelet. Every Sunday morning, my grandmother is happy to cook the omelet for me and I am happy to eat it.

Ingredients

- 8-10 eggs
- 2 red bell peppers
- 200 gms sausage
- 100 gms hard cheese
- ½ bunch of spring onion
- Vegetable oil for frying
- Black ground pepper to taste
- Salt to taste

Stages of Cooking

1. Wash bell peppers, cut them in halves, and remove the seeds. Chop the bell peppers. Dice sausage and combine it with bell peppers. Preheat vegetable oil and fry the ingredients slightly.
2. Grate hard cheese. Rinse and cut spring onion finely. Add the cheese and onion to the frying pan.
3. Beat and whip the eggs. Pour the egg mass above the ingredients in the pan. Cover with lid and cook the eggs until done.

Traditional Ukrainian Meat Dishes

Rice Pilaf (*Plov*)

Submitted by Solomia Kernytska

This is my mom, Natalia Kernytska's recipe.

Ingredients

- 500 gms (1 lb) meat
- 400 gms rice
- 1 carrot
- 2 medium onions
- Salt to taste
- Pepper to taste
- Oil (for frying onion, carrot, and meat)

Stages of Cooking

1. Fry the meat in a large, deep pan.
2. Add chopped carrot and onions; fry.
3. Wash the rice. Fill the pan with water and put the rice into it. Let it cook for 15 to 20 minutes. Add cooked rice to pan with fried meat, carrot, and onion.
4. Cook the whole mixture with rice for 25 minutes.
5. Mix all the ingredients gently.

Fried Chicken

Submitted by Maria Hirnyk

I am 16 years old. I live in Dobromyl. My favorite dish is fried chicken. This recipe is from my mom, Lesya Hirnyk.

Ingredients

- 1 chicken, cut into pieces
- 3 tsp salt
- ½ tsp fresh black pepper
- ½ tsp paprika
- 2 cups flour
- 3/4 cup vegetable shortening
- 1/8 tsp cayenne pepper
- Buttermilk

Stages of Cooking

1. Rinse the chicken and dry with paper towels. In a large bowl, combine the buttermilk, 1 tsp salt, 1/4 tsp each of black pepper and paprika.
2. Add the chicken pieces and turn to coat. Cover and refrigerate at least 2 hours, turning the pieces occasionally.
3. Combine the flour and remaining salt, black pepper, paprika, and cayenne.
4. Put the shortening in a large frying pan and melt over medium/high heat.
5. Remove the chicken from the buttermilk and drain well.
6. Dredge the chicken pieces in the flour mixture and shake off the excess.
7. Place the chicken skin-side down in the hot pan. Do not move the chicken until the coating is set, 4 to 6 minutes.
8. When the underside is deep golden brown, turn the chicken over and fry on the second side until also deep golden brown.

Chicken Kiev

Submitted by Solomia Hyz

Ingredients

- 130 gms (5 oz) chicken breast
- 20 gms (1 oz) butter
- 2 gms (1/4 oz) fresh dill, chopped fine
- Salt and white pepper to taste
- 1 egg
- 50 gms (2 oz) breadcrumbs
- 100 ml (3.5 oz) oil

Stages of Cooking

1. Remove the bones from the chicken.
2. Put the fillet in plastic wrap and pound to even thickness.
3. Season the fillet with salt and pepper.
4. Combine butter and dill and spread on fillet.
5. Roll the fillet and fasten the edges.
6. Beat the egg; dip the fillet in the egg and then into the breadcrumbs.
7. Fry the rolled fillet in the oil until brown on all sides.
8. Put the fillet on a try and bake 15 minutes until the meat is cooked through.

Marinated Baked Ham

Submitted by Solomia Hyz

Ingredients

- 200 gms (7 oz) onion
- 50 gms (1.5 oz) garlic
- 900 gms (2 lbs) pork fillet
- 700 gms (.5 liter) kvas
- 1 oz vinegar
- 5 gms (1/4 oz) fresh mint
- 1 bay leaf
- Salt and black pepper to taste

Stages of Cooking

1. Peel and finely chop the onion and garlic.
2. Make little slices in the meat and fill pockets with onion and garlic mixture.
3. Generously season the pork with salt and pepper.
4. Put the pork in a bowl, add enough *kvas* to cover, and season with vinegar, mint, and bay leaf.
5. Cover and refrigerate overnight.
6. Bake in a 200c oven for 40-60 minutes, or until golden.

Pork Rolls Filled with Mushrooms

Submitted by Solomia Hyz

Ingredients

- 500 gms (1 lb) pork fillet
- 100 gms (3.5 oz) carrot
- 100 gms (3.5 oz) onion
- 400 gms (14 oz) mushrooms
- 3 tbsp oil
- 1 cup meat stock
- Salt and black pepper to taste

Stages of Cooking

1. Cut the pork into 1 cm (1/2 in) slices and pound to even thickness. Season each piece with salt and pepper.
2. Peel and chop the onion and carrot. Fry in oil until soft.
3. Chop the mushrooms and add to the vegetables. Continue frying until vegetables are lightly browned.
4. Add a spoonful of vegetables to pork slices, roll, and secure with a toothpick.
5. Fry rolls in oil until browned, and place in large casserole.
6. Add meat broth, cover pot, and cook over very low heat for 45 minutes.

Traditional Ukrainian Fish Dishes

Dressed Herring

Submitted by Olexandra Mrachynska

Ingredients

- 700 gms (1 1/2 lbs) herring
- 3 boiled potatoes
- 2 boiled carrots
- 3 boiled beet roots
- 2 boiled eggs
- 1 onion
- 200 gms (7 oz) mayonnaise
- Salt to taste

Stages of Cooking

1. Discard the skin and bones from the herring and chop the fish.
2. Peel and grate the vegetables and the eggs in separate bowls.
3. In a tall glass bowl, spread a layer of herring on the bottom.
4. Then put the onions and potatoes and add a layer of mayonnaise.
5. Then put the carrots, more mayonnaise, followed by beet root and more mayonnaise.
6. Top with grated eggs.
7. Cover and place in refrigerator overnight.

Herring

Submitted by Andriy Voitovych

My grandmother is very industrious. She prepares a lot of tasty food. My grandmother's name is Orysia. The herring has a wonderful flavor and can be served with mashed potatoes. The herring can also be served at New Year's as a salad with black bread — Herring Under a Fur Coat.

Ingredients
- 2 frozen herring
- ½ liter (17 oz) water
- 2 tbsp salt
- 1.5 tbsp sugar
- 1 tsp mustard powder
- 1 bay leaf
- 4-5 scented pepper
- 1 clove
- 2 onions
- Greens to taste
- 2 tbsp oil

Stages of Cooking
1. Mix water, salt, sugar, mustard powder, bay leaf, scented pepper, and clove.
2. Put on fire and bring to a boil.
3. Turn off the fire and leave mixture to cool completely.
4. Add prepared herring to the marinade and let stand for 12-14 hours.
5. Sprinkle with chopped onion, greens, and oil when serving.

Pizza

Pizza Recipe #1

Submitted by Ada Bilousova

This is my mom's recipe. My mom's name is Liliya Bilousova.

Ingredients

Dough
- 400 gms (14 oz) flour
- 125 gms (4 1/2 oz) margarine, melted
- 150 gms (5 oz) milk
- 50 gms (1 1/2 oz) yeast

Topping
- 100-120 gms tomato sauce
- 150-180 gms mushrooms
- 6 black olives, sliced
- 150 gms hard cheese
- Oil

Stages of Cooking

1. Mix flour and margarine into warmed milk.
2. Add yeast to the flour and milk.
3. Put the dough in the refrigerator for 20 minutes.
4. Pour a little oil on the surface of the form for baking.
5. Lay out the dough, spread on the tomato sauce, mushrooms, olives, and cheese.
6. Place in the preheated oven (180 degrees) and bake for 15-20 minutes, until the cheese has melted.

Pizza Recipe #2

Submitted by Anastasia Pynylo

A favorite recipe of my Grandmother Luba.

Ingredients

- 300 ml (10 oz) milk
- 2 tbsp oil
- 1 package fast yeast
- 490 gms flour
- Salt to taste
- Toppings can be ham, sausage, or mushrooms
- Ketchup
- Cheese

Stages of Cooking

1. Pour yeast in a bowl, salt it, and add warm milk.
2. Add a little flour and beat the liquid dough.
3. Add oil.
4. Mix and pour small amounts of flour until the dough becomes thick.
5. Leave the dough for 15 minutes in a warm place.
6. Roll the dough and shape it into a form (round).
7. Cover the dough with ketchup, lay on ham, sausage, or mushrooms.
8. Sprinkle cheese on top.
9. Preheat oven to 180c (350f) degrees.
10. Bake the pizza in a well-heated oven for 20-30 minutes until ready.

Pizza Recipe #3

Submitted by Solomia Kernytska

This is another recipe of my mom.

Ingredients

- 1 cup flour
- 25 gms (1 oz) yeast
- 1 egg
- 1/2 cup milk
- Salt to taste
- 100 gms (3.5 oz) ham
- 100 gms (3.5 oz) cheese
- 100 gms (3.5 oz) mushroom

Stages of Cooking

1. Mix flour, yeast, egg, milk, and salt.
2. Knead the dough.
3. Preheat oven to 350 degrees with rack in lower position. On a baking sheet lined with parchment paper, stretch out dough to a 16-by-10-inch rectangle.
4. Put ham and mushrooms on the top and sprinkle with chopped cheese.
5. Bake at 200c (390f) degrees for 15-20 minutes.

Donuts

Donut Recipe #1

Submitted by Kateryna Voloshyn

Donuts are usually prepared for Christmas. They are among 12 Lent dishes of the Holy Supper.

Ingredients

- 100 gms (3.5 oz) sugar
- 100 gms (3.5 oz) oil for dough
- 100 gms (3.5 oz) water
- 50 gms (1.5 oz) yeast
- ½ kg (17.5 oz) flour
- 2 eggs
- 1/2 liter (17 oz) oil for frying
- Powdered sugar

Stages of Cooking

1. Mix sugar, 100 gms of oil, and hot water. Cool.
2. Pour into a 1/2 liter jar, add cold water to fill the jar.
3. Add 50 gms of yeast and cook on the countertop for 5 to 10 minutes.
4. Combine 1/2 kg of flour and two eggs and mix into the yeast solution.
5. Slowly mix the flour until the dough is softened.
6. Cut a piece of dough, roll it, and then cut into pieces.
7. Shape into round pancakes. You can make a hole and add jam to the donuts.
8. Sprinkle flour on a board and then lay the donuts on the board.
9. Put the board in a warm place and wait for the donuts to grow.
10. Put 1/2 liter of oil in a pan. Bring to a boil and drop 5 or 6 donuts into the oil.
11. Roll the donuts over so all sides get browned, then remove them from the oil.
12. Sprinkle with powdered sugar.

Donut Recipe #2

Submitted by Victoria Voloshyn

My Grandmother's name is Maria. I really like her cooking. My favorite dish that my grandmother prepares is donuts. A family tradition is to make donuts at Christmas. My grandmother makes the donuts every Christmas, which takes a lot of effort. Good appetite!

Ingredients

- 350 gms (12 oz) milk
- 1 egg
- 70 gms (2.5 oz) butter, melted
- Pinch sugar
- ½ tsp salt
- 20 gms (1 oz) fresh yeast
- Frying oil
- 1 tsp lemon zest
- 550 gms (1 lb, 3 oz) wheat flour
- 13 gms vanilla sugar powder

Stages of Cooking

1. Mix milk, egg, butter, and pinch sugar.
2. Stir until the sugar is dissolved.
3. Add salt and heat mixture up to 38-40c (100f) degrees.
4. Add yeast and lemon zest to mixture.
5. Apply flour to the mixture and knead dough.
6. The dough should be soft and light.
7. Cover the dough with a damp towel and leave it in a warm place for an hour and a half.
8. Spread the dough on a board to thickness of 2.25 cm (1 in).
9. Use a glass to cut out the donuts.

10. Lay them on a board smeared with a thin layer of flour. Cover them with a towel and leave in a warm place for 15-20 minutes.
11. Deep fry on both sides until golden color. Put on paper napkins so that the oil is absorbed from the donuts. Sprinkle on all sides with vanilla sugar powder.

Donut Recipe #3

Submitted by Diana Savko

This is my grandmother's recipe. Her name is Oksana. She is a great chef. Enjoy your meal!

Ingredients

Dough
- 1 cup milk
- 1 tbsp sugar
- 2 tbsp vegetable oil
- 40 gms (1.5 oz) yeast
- 400 gms (14 oz) flour
- 2 eggs

Filling
Choose the filling according to your taste. I use strawberry jam.

Stages of Cooking

We will make the dough. It is the most important part of the recipe.

1. Mix the milk and flour. If possible, milk should have fat — preferably whole milk. The milk and flour mixture should be warm.
2. Add the yeast, sugar, and oil. Knead the dough until it is soft.
4. Roll the dough and cut into 5 millimeter (1/4 inch).
5. Insert filling into the dough and cover the filling with the second half of the dough.
6. Use a cup to squeeze the donuts.
7. Fry in a large pot filled with vegetable oil for a few minutes on each side.
8. Do this until the dough and filling are finished.

Desserts

Cottage Cheese Pancakes (*Symyky*)

Submitted by Olexandra Mrachynska

Ingredients

- 600 gms (1 lb, 5 oz) cottage cheese
- 4 tbsp sugar
- ½ tsp salt
- 3 eggs
- 50 gms (2 oz) raisins
- 3-4 tbsp oil
- 2-3 tbsp flour

Stages of Cooking

1. Combine the cottage cheese, eggs, sugar, and salt.
2. Stir in the flour.
3. Rinse and drain the raisins, then add to the cottage cheese mix.
4. Form egg-sized balls and then flatten into pancakes.
5. Fry in oil until golden on both sides.

Charlotke

Submitted by Ada Bilousova

This is my grandmother's recipe.

Ingredients

- 200 gms (7 oz) sugar
- 5 eggs
- 1 cup sour cream
- 3 cups flour or breadcrumbs
- 2 tsp baking powder
- 3-4 apples
- Butter
- Vanilla sugar to taste

Stages of Cooking

1. Mix eggs with sugar.
2. Add in sour cream, flour, and baking powder.
3. The apples are washed and cut into thin slices.
4. Grease the baking dish with butter, sprinkle with flour or breadcrumbs. Pour in the batter and spread evenly. Spread the fruit filling on top.
5. Preheat the oven to 180 degrees and bake for 35-40 minutes.
6. The finished *charlotke* is sprinkled with powdered sugar.

Pumpkin Dough

Submitted by Anastasia Pynylo

I am 11 years old. I live in Dobromyl. I have a granny. Her name is Luba. She is very hardworking and prepares very tasty recipes. Here is one of her recipes. This dough can also be used with an apricot filling or strawberry jam. My favorite ones are filled with pumpkin and poppy.

Ingredients

- 1 liter (1 qt) milk
- 100 gms (3.5 oz) yeast
- 50 gms (1.5 oz) butter
- 2 eggs
- 1 1/2 glass sugar
- 15 gms (1/2 oz) vanilla sugar
- 1 kg (2 lbs) flour
- Oil

Stages of Cooking

1. In warm milk, dissolve the yeast.
2. Add sugar, eggs, butter, and flour.
3. Leave the dough in a warm place for 1 hour to grow.
4. Roll the dough out to 1 cm (1/2 in).
5. Cut the dough into circles.
6. Put a stuffing in the dough.
7. Fill the edges.
8. Form into a ball.
9. Leave to grow on the table for 30 minutes.
10. Fry in hot oil.

Fruit Ice Cream

Submitted by Nadia Belei

My favorite dessert is fruit ice cream. I like cooking it.

Ingredients

- 250-300 ml (8.5 oz-14 oz) cream
- 150 ml (5 oz) condensed milk
- 1 banana
- 150 gms (5 oz) strawberries

Stages of Cooking

1. Mix banana, strawberries, and condensed milk.
2. Shake the cream until it becomes lush.
3. Mix cream with fruit mixture.
4. Pour into plastic cups.
5. Put in freezer for 3 hours.

Ice Cream

Submitted by Nadia Belei

Cooking ice cream is my hobby. This recipe is mine.

Ingredients

- 200 ml (6.5 oz) sour cream
- 100-150 ml (3.5 oz-5 oz) condensed milk
- 1 tsp vanilla essence
- 80 gms (3 oz) chocolate

Stages of Cooking

1. Shake the sour cream until it becomes lush.
2. Add condensed milk and vanilla essence.
3. Put in the mixer on a low speed.
4. Melt chocolate.
5. Cover the sides of 4-5 paper cups with chocolate.
6. Wait 4 minutes.
7. Pour ice cream into the paper cups.
8. Put in the freezer overnight.

Holiday Recipes

Traditional Beverage (*Uzvar*)

Submitted by Olexandra Mrachynska

Ingredients

- 200 gms (7 oz) dried apples
- 100 gms (3.5 oz) raisins
- 300 gms (10.5 oz) dried pears
- 200 gms (7 oz) prunes
- 2 liter (1/2 gallon) boiling water
- 250 gms (9 oz) honey
- 1 cinnamon stick
- piece of orange peel

Stages of Cooking

1. Rinse dried fruits in cold water; drain.
2. Combine fruits with boiling water and cook gently for 30 minutes.
3. Add the honey, cinnamon stick, and orange peel and allow to rest, covered, for several hours.
4. Remove the fruits and serve separately. Discard the cinnamon stick and orange peel. Serve the liquid cool.

Cereal Dish #1 (*Kutya*)

Submitted by Olexandra Mrachynska

Kutya is mostly served at Christmas celebrations. *Kutya* is a main dish of the Holy Supper.

Ingredients

- 2 cups cooked wheat
- 6 tbsp ground poppy seeds
- ¼ cup honey
- ¼ cup roughly chopped walnuts
- 100 gms (3.5 oz) raisins
- Salt to taste
- Sugar to taste

Stages of Cooking

1. Wash and soak the wheat in cold water overnight.
2. Next morning bring wheat to a boil and simmer for 2 hours, until kernels burst open.
3. Cover the poppy seeds with hot water and simmer for 3 to 5 minutes. Drain; grind twice using the finest blade in a food chopper.
4. Add ground poppy seeds to wheat.
5. Combine honey and a little sugar in a little hot water. Add to wheat.
6. Add the roughly chopped walnuts and salt to taste when serving.

Cereal Dish #2 (*Kutya*)

Submitted by Yulia Chura

This is my mom's recipe. Cooking this traditional holiday cereal dish is a difficult thing. So that the meal is successful and the wheat is boiled correctly, it is necessary to cook it for a long time and also to pre-soak in cold water overnight. You can also add raisins if you like but this is not necessary. Honey is best to sweeten the porridge.

Ingredients

- 1 cup wheat grains
- 100 gms (3.5 oz) poppy
- 100 gms (3.5 oz) walnuts
- 1-3 tbsp honey or sugar

Stages of Cooking

1. Cook the wheat grains in water until the grains are like ordinary loose porridge.
2. Let the wheat grains cool.
3. Sweeten the wheat grains to taste with sugar.
4. Mix poppy and honey and add to the wheat.
5. If porridge is thick, it can be diluted with cooled boiled water.

Cereal Dish #3 (*Kutya*)

Submitted by Nadia Belei

I like drawing and cooking. I love my grandmother very much. Her name is Miroslava Karaman. She is good and smart. I also like when my granny is cooking and, most of all, I like this dish. This is an old family recipe.

Ingredients

- 1 cup wheat
- 100 gm (3.5 oz) poppy
- 1-2 tablespoons melted honey
- ½ cup chopped walnuts
- 80-100 gms raisins

Stages of Cooking

1. Soak the wheat overnight.
2. In the morning, put on a low heat and cook until ready (1 hour).
3. Add crushed poppy, nuts, and raisins.
4. Mix and add melted honey.

Mushroom and Onion Dumplings (*Vushka*)

Submitted by Ada Bilousova

This is my grandmother's recipe.

Ingredients

Dough
- 300 gms (7 oz) flour
- 1 egg
- 120 ml water or milk
- ¼ tsp salt
- 1 1/2 glasses water

Stuffing
- 250-260 gms mushrooms and onions
- 1 tbsp oil
- Salt and pepper to taste

Stages of Cooking

1. Cook the mushrooms (1 hour).
2. Fry onion until tender. Add chopped mushrooms and cook the mixture about 10 minutes. Remove from heat and allow mixture to cool. Add salt and pepper.
3. Knead the dough.
4. Cut circles from the dough using a glass.
5. Inside the circle put a bit of stuffing.
6. Fold the circle in half and press the edges of the dough with your fingers.
7. Boil in salted water for 2 to 4 minutes.

Sugar Cookies

Submitted by Sofia Ledakhivska

My grandmother is a very sweet person. She likes me very much and takes care of my brother and me. I got this recipe from her. My grandmother cooks very well. My grandmother also teaches us clean habits. My granny is beautiful and a great inspiration to me. I love her very much.

Ingredients

- 250 gms (8.5 oz) cream cheese, softened
- 1 cup butter, softened
- 2 tbsp sugar
- 25 gms (1 oz) vanilla extract
- 2 cups flour
- 4 tbsp colored sugar

Stages of Cooking

1. Beat the cream cheese and butter together in a large bowl with a mixer.
2. Add sugar and vanilla extract and mix well.
3. Gradually add flour, beating well.
4. Refrigerate for 3 hours.
5. Roll out the dough and cut into shapes with cookie cutters.
6. Sprinkle with colored sugar.
7. Bake at 180c (350f) degrees for 10-15 minutes.

www.ingramcontent.com/pod-product-compliance
Lightning Source LLC
Chambersburg PA
CBHW031202160426
43193CB00008B/474